TELL YOUR STORY

Jess,

Thanks so much for
taking a look. Let me
know what you think.

by China McCarney

For my dad. On my 31st birthday and on the day you retire. Thank you for continuing to tell your story and encouraging me to tell mine.

My story is what it is because of you.

02/24/2018

Contents

Introduction

*"Courage is to tell the story of who
you are with your whole heart."*
- Brene Brown

Your Story.

How is it told? Who is it told by? If you told your story from your birth to this point in your life, what would you say?

Are you uncomfortable thinking about these answers? If so, good. If not, good.

There is no perfect story. There is no perfect life. Unfortunately, with the current capabilities we have to present ourselves and our lives with technology, we can share only what we deem share-worthy. We can create an image of perfection to all of our friends and peers on Twitter, Instagram, Facebook, you name it.

Are there consequences to this? I firmly believe so.

With increasing technological advances we have more access to each other's lives than ever before. This is great of course because we can stay involved in each other's lives from afar. We can keep up with anyone and everyone. It is like a constant, continuous, high school reunion. However, we are also capable of filtering what we want and do not want to share about our lives.

Trip to Europe: SHARE. Marital problems: DON'T SHARE. Job Promotion: SHARE.

Mental Health Issues: DON'T SHARE. The list goes on and on and on.

We are constantly filtering out the negative and sharing, for the most part, the positive and big experiences in our lives. This creates a false societal standard that makes everyone feel like they have to live up to it. I know people that do things or go to events just for a picture that they can post on Social Media. This is creating an extremely anxious and depressed society because people have a false belief that everyone's lives are perfect. You want the next big photo. You want to go on the best and most elaborate big trip. You want to hide any negative battle you are going through because no one would dare post or share about that. We are fighting with everything we have to never admit we are going through a struggle or something negative.

I want this to change. I want this to change now. I want to use my life to change this in the future. I want to share my Mental Health Battle as an example of the power of Telling Your Story. Your true story.

Why? I want to help create a community, a society and a social norm where we are allowed to be 100% ourselves. I want us all to be brave enough to share our TRUE STORY instead of what we think people should hear or should see. The harder we fight to keep the negatives and battles in the dark, the worse they will get.

This change can not be accomplished by one person. This

change can only occur if there are enough people willing to take action. The action necessary: people willing to be 100% of themselves and share their story. ALL of their story. Not just the good parts. Not just the sexy, exotic picture on Social Media. The good, the bad and the ugly is what needs to be shared to create a genuine community and a true story society.

No more false presentations of perfection. No more hiding or being ashamed of our "imperfections". Let's create a community and society of togetherness and rid the stigma attached to battles that so many of us fight. Instead of pointing the finger in blame, let's point the finger in love. Instead of being ashamed to ask for help, let's embrace the beauty of the resources and support that is available to ALL OF US.

Let us believe that our story matters and we can all BE THE CHANGE!

China McCarney

CHAPTER 1
My Story

*"There is no greater agony than bearing
an untold story inside you."*
- Maya Angelou

The quote above by Maya Angelou hits me hard right in the chest. I had an untold story inside of me for much of my life. I bottled up emotions, built as many psychological walls as I could, and worst of all I hid a mental health battle I was struggling with for years. I presented my life the same way most of us do: I presented the image of a successful athlete, life was moving along "perfectly", the future was oh so bright. All the while I felt like I was really only presenting about 75% of who I was to the outside world.

I had my first panic attack in 2009. I was forty five minutes into a three hour drive with my new girlfriend of three months and my body was suddenly consumed by symptoms I had never felt before. My heart started racing. My body felt like it was burning from the inside out and it felt like needles were poking me everywhere. I suddenly couldn't breathe. I was nauseous. I was dizzy. I felt faint. This was all occurring while I was driving and it became clear that I needed to pull off the road.

I pulled the car over and began to walk. I needed fresh air and felt that if I walked maybe I could get away from this intense feeling

I had never felt before. I had no idea what these symptoms were and at the time and I thought I could be dying. I walked for close to two hours with no regard for my girlfriend and what she may be thinking or feeling.

The panic attack won that day. My dad had to drive for over an hour to come get me while my girlfriend followed us home in my car.

The following couple of days I saw doctors and they did numerous tests to see what had happened. "Anxiety". "Stress". "Panic". Those were the words they used to describe the single most terrifying physical experience of my life. "It's all mental?" I asked. "How can all of that physical discomfort be fucking mental?".

I had no idea at the time that this event in 2009 would be the single most important event in my life.

Why share the gory details of that day? Why paint the picture as clearly as I can to describe that event in my life? The answer to both of these questions is the premise of this book. It is the willingness to share what we go through, and who we are, with 100% truth that can help us and others in multiple ways.

So what happened in the following weeks, months and years after hearing that it was all mental from a doctor? Did I seek help from counselors and try medication to improve my mental health? Absolutely not.

Did I begin to share my story with everyone to see if there were resources out there or if others went through the same thing? Absolutely not.

I went into a psychological shock. I felt guilty. I felt embarrassed. I felt ashamed. Again, I repeated the same question over and over in my head, "How can that level of physical discomfort be fucking mental?"

There is a vital point to bring up at this stage of my story. A point that I believe we can all relate to in terms of why we present what we present about ourselves at certain times. During this period of time when I went through my first Panic Attack in 2009, I was being highly pursued by Major League Baseball organizations as a top prospect. This was a huge reason I hid so much about what I was going through. I was worried about what the outside perception would be of my mental health and what it could mean for my career and my future.

This points directly to a big problem in our society. We are so worried about the consequences of being who we truly are that we try to present ourselves in a way that will be fully accepted. This creates turmoil and angst within us. We see an image of perfection and what is acceptable through the media and on Social Media and we try to mimic it. All the while fighting the battle between presenting an "acceptable" version of ourselves and being who we truly are and pursuing what we really want to pursue.

I did not feel that I could present what I was really going through without it having a detrimental effect on my career and my relationships. I had to worry about what I was presenting to the world and who I truly was on the inside at the same time. It was exhausting. It was painful. It continued to add fuel to my mental health fire year after year until I finally reached my boiling point.

That boiling point was in 2015. I was sitting in the parking lot of the Habit Grill (shout out to their burgers) and had just had yet another Panic Attack. I was sitting in my car reflecting on the last six years of my life and talking to myself. "I can't do this shit anymore."

I started to think about what my anxiety had cost me in those six years. Countless friends. Girlfriends. My entire social life. I had convinced myself and others that I wasn't interested in a social life. I was committed to my career. I was putting my head down and setting up the rest of my life with hard work and dedication to my craft. These were all bull shit one liners I would use as a positive excuse as to why I was neglecting my personal relationships. The truth was I had designed a reclusive, comfortable lifestyle where I wouldn't put myself in any uncomfortable situations where panic or anxiety would arise.

Those moments of reflection in my car were so important because they forced me into action. I took out my phone and called a counselor to schedule my first session to talk about my mental health battle. I had that phone number for such a long time. I felt it was better to suffer in silence and hiding for six years rather than seeking help because of the possibility that others would find out that I suffered from anxiety and panic attacks.

That describes the unfortunate stigma attached to mental health issues perfectly. People are so terrified of the perception of their anxiety, depression, etc. that they would rather hide it instead of seeking help or using the resources available to them. How do we change this? We tell our story. Our true story. We embrace 100% of who we are.

I did not realize this over night. As I said, it took me six years to take the first step. However, that first step was the beginning of the greatest part of my story. I saw the counselor consistently week after week for over a year. At the beginning I held back information because I was still committed to presenting an acceptable version of myself. As the sessions went on, and I became more comfortable, I started to share everything. The embarrassing panic attacks. The lost relationships. Everything.

The counselor's perspective and professional advice helped tremendously. However, what seemed to be helping the most was me becoming more and more comfortable with the true version of myself. The real me. I continued to get more comfortable sharing my story without shame. Reflecting on my story gave me perspective that my anxiety and panic attacks were just a part of me and nothing to be ashamed of. Week after week I felt more and more weight being lifted off my shoulders. I felt lighter and more free mentally than I had in my entire adult life. Simply said, I finally felt like the real me on the inside and the outside.

I knew that this step was just the first one. In order to continue the momentum and achieve the ultimate success I needed to share my story with the same transparency and truth to everyone. My family. My friends. The world. It was absolutely daunting thinking about sharing my mental health journey with everyone. I implemented the most valuable lesson I have learned up until this point in my life: Action and step-by-step.

When we think about big tasks or a big goal often times it can be overwhelming. We almost get paralyzed and stuck before we start because we think about achieving an entire task in one shot. What has helped me tremendously is breaking tasks down into steps and attacking one at a time. The most important component is action. As long as you are taking consistent action towards your goal you will be putting yourself in a position to succeed or learn from failures. I can not stand when people talk about what they are going to do, what they are going to accomplish, what improvements they want in their life, and yet they never put in the work or take the action.

You want success? Take fucking action.

My first action was reaching out to family and friends and explaining why I had changed over the years. I apologized for becoming a recluse and not being my former social self. I explained the physical symptoms I go through and how at times they can be unbearable. Of course, most of my family and friends were beyond understanding and a lot of them expressed that they also dealt with some form of a mental health struggle. The positive part of the journey continued and I could not believe the power that telling my story was having on me and on others.

My second action was wanting to do something big for anxiety and depression. I wanted to share with everyone that by sharing my story, and being my genuine self, I had improved my quality of life and my mental health. I wanted to share that by finally accepting it and presenting it to the world, my mental health struggles were no longer a negative attribute for me that I hid. They were just a part of me that I was willing to talk about. This second action was a Social Media campaign that would change the course of my entire life.

It was October of 2016 and I was having second thoughts about doing an Anxiety and Depression Campaign in November to raise awareness and funds. It was a perfectly timed conversation with my friend Jon Spendlove that put me over the hump to follow through and make the campaign happen. What would occur over those thirty days in November of 2016 would change my life forever and show me my true purpose.

I posted videos throughout the month telling my story about my battle with anxiety and panic attacks. I told the story in a very matter of fact, positive way and explained that I would no longer be held captive by the stigma attached to anxiety and depression. I encouraged others to tell their story and to embrace all of who they were because of the immense positive change it had created for me. The response was incredible.

I will never forget my phone for those thirty days. Yes, my phone. It absolutely exploded. People reaching out and wanting to share what they had gone through. People thanking me for being brave enough to open this door and share my story. People wanting to do interviews and have me on podcasts. It was incredible. Those thirty days were the culmination of six years of hiding, taking the first step to share with a counselor, sharing with my family and friends, and ultimately sharing with everyone on Social Media where I had previously presented a "perfect" image of life.

Those thirty days showed me that my story and this cause needed to be much more than a thirty day social media journey. It needed to be my life's journey and it need to be professionally handled. I reached out to a law firm shortly after the campaign to take the next action of creating a fully functioning foundation. Four short months later, after a lot of paperwork, patience and action, I received the letter in the mail that the Athletes Against Anxiety and Depression Foundation had been approved by the government and we had 501(c)(3) status. My eyes teared up as I reflected on what that letter signified. My journey and battle with mental health had shifted from embarrassment, guilt, and hiding the truth, to pride, acceptance and wanting to help others more than worrying about my day-to-day symptoms.

This is my story. It is far from over and I love each new chapter every day. I share this story as the first chapter of this book because it exemplifies my message. By telling my true story with gory details I help myself reflect on it, learn from it and realize how far I have come. More important than that, my story has helped others realize the power in telling their story and how much it can help them and others in their circle. That is the type of exponential effect where real change occurs. People coming together encouraging each other to be the real version of themselves.

We may not always understand what someone is going through and you may not have experienced a mental health battle as I have in my story. However, the principles and lessons apply to every story. There are lessons to learn from each and every story if we are willing to look and listen. There are lessons in our story for ourselves and for others if we are willing to share it with 100% truth.

That is my story with 100% truth. I am who I am now with 100% commitment to my genuine self. My story matters and it is time for you to accept and believe that YOUR STORY MATTERS as well!

Tell Your Story

China McCarney

CHAPTER 2

Your Story Matters

"Don't be ashamed of your story, it will inspire others."
- Anonymous

There is one truth that you need to realize when it comes to your story. One fact that is universally true for all of us. No matter where you've been, what you think you have or haven't done, there is one thing you need to realize right now at this moment: YOUR STORY MATTERS. It matters for yourself. It matters for others.

Everything you have done in the past and everything you have gone through is why you are where you are. Your current life is the product of all the decisions you have made up until this point. Why is this important? It is important because we have to accept all the decisions we have made in the past. They can not be changed. We should not want to change them. We should accept that they have already occurred and the only purpose they serve now is that they can teach us and others valuable lessons.

That is the power in our story. If we are willing to look, there are tremendous lessons in most of what we have gone through. From this moment on I want you to look at events in your life in one of two ways: successes to build off of or failures to learn from. It really is that simple. If you start to look at everything through one of those two lenses, you will start to see there are no catastrophic occurrences that you can't get over. Negative events in your life will stop stinging for as long as they do. You will simply take the lesson from that event and move on. You will also not rest on your success. You will start to pull the attributes and actions from each success and start to build on them and create momentum in your life.

I want to stop here and point to the key to this new two-part outlook working in your life.

Any guesses? Want to take a moment to come up with some answers in your head?

It starts with SELF. Self-reflection. Self-honesty. Self-responsibility. Self-discipline.

In order for you to build off success and learn lessons from mistakes you have to be willing to self-reflect. You have to look at the course of your life and search for the lessons yourself. You, and you alone, know your true story and if you are honest with yourself you know what you need to do to be successful. You know what you need to avoid to make less mistakes. However, you can only 100% benefit from this if you are 100% honest with yourself. It is your responsibility to be disciplined enough to constantly self-reflect and learn from what you have gone through and what you go through on a daily basis.

This is the foundation for a STORY THAT MATTERS. Honesty. Truth. Responsibility. If you implement words and attributes like these while telling your story to yourself, you can't help but benefit from the lessons you have learned throughout your life. If you implement words and attributes like these while telling your story to others, they can't help but benefit from your honesty and your willingness to share your genuine story and your genuine lessons.

If you can't tell yet, there is a theme beginning to build here. In order for your story to be as beneficial as possible, to yourself and to others, you have to take the responsibility to tell your 100% true story.

I failed at this for years. I hid my mental health struggles from everyone and paid the price with the loss of exceptional humans in my life. I made up excuses like my commitment to my career as to why I was secluding myself and pushing the world away. This was not my true story and no one, including myself, was benefiting from me withholding truth.

What are you withholding from people that is hurting yourself and/or others?

What excuses are you telling yourself and to others as to why things aren't the way you want them, the way they should be?

How much longer will you tell yourself that your story doesn't matter and there is no reason to tell your true story?

I love these types of questions because they force us into the self-reflection we need to get closer to change. The type of change that will make huge impacts on not only our lives but on the lives of so many others. Can you make the leap to be 100% your true self? Can you be brave enough to fill in the gaps of your story that you have been holding back?

I know you can do it. I've seen it. I've seen it in my journey over the past 8 years and continue to see it in my battles. I have seen it with so many others willing to share their story. If you are honest with yourself, you know you can do it too. It is about taking the first step and taking the first action. If you really want to BE THE CHANGE you wish to see in your life, and in the world, it is time to start NOW.

Remember, YOUR STORY MATTERS and it is time to tell your TRUE STORY!

Tell Your Story

China McCarney

CHAPTER 3

Only a True Story

"Strange as it may seem, my life is based on a true story."
- Ashleigh Brilliant

The effectiveness of your story relies on your level of honesty. The more you hold back or hide, the bigger the disservice you do to yourself and to others.

This is something I struggled with immensely as I started to deal with mental health issues. As i stated before, when I first started to deal with anxiety and panic attacks my natural instinct was to seclude myself from everyone and to hide what I was dealing with at all costs. When I look back and analyze why my actions were what they were, it is clear to me that I was worried about external views and societal standards more than I was worried about myself and my story. I was worried about what others thought. I was worried about what societal standards were about mental health issues. I was worried about all of that more than I was worried about getting well or getting help.

This is something we can all relate to. On some level, even if some of us want to be stubborn and not admit it, we care a great deal about what others think. We seek affirmation, acceptance and praise. We all want to be loved. This is not all bad but it can start to consume us. We can get so consumed by seeking the approval of others that we abandon everything that we believe in and everything that we aspire to be. In a way, we abandon our true story.

This can not be. This can not happen.

How can we expect to achieve our greatest results if we are not telling our whole truth? How can we take advantage of the resources and advice out there if we do not offer 100% of whatever it is that we are going through?

We miss out on so many opportunities because of our unwillingness to share the vulnerable parts of ourselves. The sad part about this is a lot of times the best advice and opportunities come when we are our most genuine selves. We get the most impactful direction from others when we share what we are truly going through.

In layman's terms, if we truly want the benefits of the resources available in the world, we have to be willing to share our true story. 100% truth for 100% results. That is the way to absorb and implement help from the outside-in.

Now what about help from the inside-out?

We take our most impactful action when we are truly honest with ourselves about what needs to change in our life for us to achieve what it is that we want to achieve.

That is a long, drawn out sentence that can easily be passed by. We can easily say what the fuck did I just read, not understand, and move on. That would be a mistake and it would be a mistake for me to not segment it and break it down.

"We take our most impactful action when we are truly honest with ourselves…" If we stop there, and break that down, we can begin to learn what I believe is one of the most valuable lessons in life.

How often are you truly honest with yourself? How often do you reflect on what you are trying to achieve in life? Do you hold yourself accountable for what happens in your life instead of pointing the finger at others or circumstances as to why you are not where you want to be?

The simple truth is that we have the answers to most of our questions inside of us. The issue is we do not want to accept that truth because we feel it is easier to hold onto an excuse or blame an external factor as to why we are falling short. We do not tell ourselves our true story so we can not fully take genuine action towards what we are trying to achieve.

"…what needs to change in our life for us to achieve what it is that we want to achieve." If you accept that you have what it takes to change your life, you will be able to change your life. It is that simple and I know that is tough to hear. You know what you need to change in your life on a daily basis to get closer to where you want to go. You know what does not add value to your life. You know what and who you need to eliminate from your life. The problem is this simplicity and this truth scares us.

Why? Because we have been trained to accept a societal standard story instead of our true story. We have gotten so external that it feels foreign or uncomfortable to follow our true instincts and our gut. Social media has created this rat race of perfection that it is almost impossible not to compare or compete behind the screen of an iphone.

Make a commitment to yourself today. What makes you you? What is your true story? Share that with the world. Use that genuine version of yourself to soak up the world's resources. Commit to the mindset that YOU CAN be the change you wish to see in your life. It starts with authenticity and the change occurs with action. The action: from this moment on you will commit to live from the inside-out and tell the world your true story. You will not tell the standard story that you think society wants to hear. You will not shy away from what makes you you. You will embrace ALL of you and BE YOUR OWN CHANGE you wish to see in your life and in the world.

Tell Your Story

China McCarney

CHAPTER 4
Standard Story

*"Until the lion learns how to write,
every story will glorify the hunter."*
- African Proverb

I want us to look at what most of us do when we tell our stories. Remember, telling our stories doesn't only mean verbally telling it to someone out loud. Telling our story is what we are doing inside of our heads at all times. All of our thoughts about ourselves. All of our thoughts about what other people are saying or thinking about us. These thoughts are all contributing to what our story is and how we present it to the outside world.

Most of us only share what we believe is going to paint the best picture of ourselves. I call this our Standard Story.

The standard story happens everywhere. It happens in all walks of life. You see it all the time in the media. We are told what our story should be. We are told what to buy. We are told what to look like and how we should dress. This may actually be one of the worst times in our history in terms of the standard story being thrown in our face and us being exposed to biased information.

Think about the countless ways we are now exposed to advertisements, biased recommendations and celebrity branding, all telling us to be or feel a certain way. Everytime we open our phones, turn on the tv or drive down the street, we see things telling us what to do or how to feel.

One of my favorite examples of the standard story is watching celebrities or athletes during interviews. They all sound like robots that have been programmed to say a few lines so that they don't get in trouble with the media or with their fans. It is very rare where you see a genuine answer about how someone really feels. The sad part is, when someone does share what they are really feeling, they get destroyed in the media and by social media trolls.

What does that teach us? Even if it is subconscious, we learn to hold back from what we really feel or what we are really going through. We learn a few things we can repeat to be accepted in society. We learn what is "acceptable". We do not learn to be who we really are.

How do we change this? How do we flip the programming and start standing up for who we really are?

It starts with awareness. We have to be aware of the story that we are telling. We have to be aware of the reasons we are telling the story a certain way. That awareness starts when you make a conscious decision to start paying attention to what is contributing to your story. You then have to determine if those contributing factors are genuine or are they the standard story that has been projected onto you by society and other external factors.

The second half of the awareness after determining what external factors have contributed to your story over time is determining what your inner dialogue is to yourself about your story. Our internal dialogue to ourselves is much different from our external dialogue to others. We are constantly fighting to present our standard story in a way that will benefit us or paint the proper picture instead of sharing the whole truth.

I want you to take a moment right now to think about your average internal dialogue. Is it positive? Is it negative? Does it even closely resemble what you share with your loved ones or people that you talk to?

There are no wrong answers to these questions. That is the beauty of it. You just took the first step in being aware as to why your story is what it is. The more often you ask yourself these types of questions, the more often you can call yourself out if you are not presenting your true story and presenting a standard story. The more often you ask yourself these questions, the more often you'll analyze what you want your story to be. You will start to recognize when you are not being your true self or standing up for what you believe in.

The change just occured. The awareness just began. Just by you asking yourself those questions and reflecting on the answers you begin to get a better feel for your story and the authenticity of that story. The key to sustained success is the consistent discipline to reflect this way on a regular basis. It is like anything else in life, the more you put into it the more you will get out of it. If you want to consistently tell your true story you have to continue to ask yourself questions and be honest about the answers.

Just by being aware you can guard against the standard story. You can begin to tell your story from the inside out. You will start to give external factors less and less power and the true you and your true story will begin to shine. Make the commitment to no longer tell the standard story. TELL YOUR STORY for you. TELL YOUR STORY for others.

Tell Your Story

China McCarney

CHAPTER 5

Accept Your Story

"Accept yourself as you are right now; an imperfect, changing, growing and worthy person."
- Denis Waitley

"Accept yourself as you are right now."

Let that sink in.

Can you do that? Can you accept everything you've ever done? Can you embrace who you are today?

In order to be who you are really meant to be, you have to.

You have to accept yourself. You have to accept where you are in life. It is an easy concept. It is extremely difficult to implement. This is the first and perhaps the most important step in moving towards your genuine self. The moment you accept yourself is the moment the external factors and judgments lose their value.

I want you to picture the way your life would look and feel if you claimed responsibility for everything that happened to you, is happening to you and will happen to you. How would it feel to look within first as opposed to looking at an external factor or circumstance to blame? It is the most amazing feeling when you begin to implement this change. When you start to feel like you have complete control of your destiny and that you can achieve any change that you want in your life with action.

I know it is the most amazing feeling because I have felt it.

When my mental health struggles began I could not have been farther from accepting my story. I hid my story. I asked the "why me" victim questions over and over. I looked externally for answers and for circumstances to blame. I analyzed people and events in my past and tried to convince myself it was their fault. I looked at things that happened on a daily basis and pointed the finger at them and as to why they were to blame for my anxiety and panic. External-external-external.

This is not a surprising, nor rare, approach when negative things begin to happen to us. We have been conditioned over time to point the finger rather than looking within. It is easier to blame others or other circumstances as to why we are not where we want to be or why some negative situation has occurred in our life. It is much harder to implement silence, responsibility and reflection within as to how you got to where you are and how you are going to get to where you want to go.

Where was I? Mental health hell.

Where did I want to go? Mental health freedom.

Remember, I spent 5 to 6 years hiding, running, blaming and not taking responsibility for my mental health journey or the changes I wanted to see. It was that panic attack in 2015 in the Habit parking lot that forced me into a different approach. It was at that moment I knew I needed to accept my story and figure out what action I needed to take to get my desired result. It was at that moment I knew from that point forward it was going to be my responsibility to create positive change in my life. It was at that moment I realized that day would be the first day of the rest of my life. I accepted my story.

I can tell from experience that these last 3 years have been the most liberating and fulfilled 3 years of my life. The beautiful part about that is these 3 years have been nowhere close to perfect. I still have panic attacks on a weekly basis. It is still extremely difficult for me to do what most people consider to be basic tasks and errands. So how the hell could these 3 years have been liberating and fulfilled? Because I accepted that this mental health battle is part of my journey. I accepted that if I take responsibility for the changes I want to see, it is all on me and external factors and judgements don't matter. I accepted that anxiety and panic attacks are just another attribute I have and I can compete like health with it and help other people.

Your story is yours and no one else's. No one can accept your story for you. No one can force you to take responsibility for every circumstance of your life. These decisions are all yours to make. Your decisions make you who you are. If you continue to make decisions based on external pressure, outside opinions and what you think is "acceptable", you will never truly live your true story. If you begin to make decisions based on your beliefs and who you truly want to be you will get closer and closer to who you truly are each and every day.

It starts now. It starts with you accepting your story. You are who you are. You are a beautiful human being with the rest of your life in front of you.

"Accept yourself as you are right now." Accept that you have control of your life. ACCEPT your story and SHARE it with the world!

Tell Your Story

China McCarney

CHAPTER 6
Accept Other's Stories

*"Accept others for who they are and for the choices
they've made even if you have difficulty understanding
their beliefs, motives and actions."*
- Anonymous

One more vital step to completing this story journey is the ability to accept other's stories without judgement. Unfortunately in today's society the opportunity to pass judgement occurs almost every second. Social media, as we talked about before, presents so many opportunities for us to judge ourselves and to judge others. Athletes are compared to other athletes. Celebrities are compared to other celebrities. Who wore it better? Who is the greatest of all time? On and on it goes in this continuous judgement cycle until it becomes the norm in society to size everyone up and compare compare compare.

As you can imagine this creates an enormous amount of anxiety and stress to keep up with everyone else. We measure ourselves against impossible societal standards and go insane in a race that we will never ever win. We are racing against the external standards and judging everyone else against those as well.

This has to change. The good news is that this change is identical to the change that pertains to your own story. We have already addressed it, and once you do it for yourself, it is much easier to do for others. The change: Accept Other's Stories.

It is not up to you to change someone else's story for them. You can give them advice and try to help in any way that you can, but at the end of the day it is their responsibility to take action to accept, change and tell their story. If you don't agree with that story you still have to accept them for them. Their story is theirs and it is not up to you what is right or wrong.

The easiest way I found to get clarity with this is to analyze it from our own story point of view. If we accept our story and commit to telling our true story, wouldn't we want people to accept our story? Even if they don't agree with our story, we would want others to accept us for us if we are truly living a genuine life and committing to telling our true story.

This is where a lot of people get in trouble with this concept. If someone's story doesn't match our version of what we want their story to be, we don't accept it. We judge it. We tear it down. We convince ourselves as to why we know what a better story for someone else is. I think a lot of this comes from us wanting to deflect our attention away from our own stories. We are unhappy about our own story so we want to attack everyone else's.

No more! Think about all of that energy you are committing to changing other's stories. Think about how rewarding it would be if you changed the allocation of that energy. Think about if you focused that energy within on changing and accepting your own story. This is a simple switch to accept other's stories and you give yourself the gift of peace and energy. You will feel this weight and burden come off of your chest the day you start to look for the positive in this world and start to accept others for who they are. You will feel a sense of lightness come over you which is the mental energy you have given yourself by not using it to attack others.

This has been an extremely tough concept for me to implement over the years. I have always been a perfectionist, highly competitive and I like to problem solve. Those attributes mixed together made me want to overhaul other's lives and make changes for people. Part of this was me deflecting the focus off of myself because I did not want to deal with my own mental health battle. Part of it was me wanting to help people but not realizing that sometimes the greatest help you can give is accepting someone for who they are. It is still a very difficult line to toe between actively helping someone and accepting them for who they are. Perhaps we can look at this a little deeper.

If someone you love or are close to has a detrimental habit that negatively affects their physical or mental health it is probably a good idea to be a little more forceful or active in trying to help them make a change. However, if someone doesn't have the same political views, nutrition habits, physical fitness routine, etc. it is not up to you to force your habits on them if those are not a priority to them. You can have a healthy conversation as to why that part of your story is that way, you can listen to their response, but at the end of the day you have to be who you are and they have to be who they are. Your story is yours and their story is theirs.

If we can all get to this place of healthy reflection with people, we can all start to allocate our energy so much more efficiently.

I like to look at it like this:

All conversations and interactions are research and education that give us life ingredients. It is up to each and every one of us to take those ingredients and to make our own recipe of who we really are. After that, we share our recipe with the world and accept other's recipes as well. Along the way we will find other ingredients from other's recipes that will help us with our life journey. No two recipes should be the exact same but we should respect and accept the work that others have done on their own recipe.

Focus each day on compassion. Think how hard you have fought to be where you are in your story. Think about how everyone else has fought hard to be where they are in their story. Think about that simple step of accepting yourself for who you are right now. Think about the same simple step that needs to be taken to accept other's stories. It is no longer your battle to fight. You will no longer waste mental energy attacking others.

You have accepted your story now it is time to accept other's stories as well.

Tell Your Story

China McCarney

CHAPTER 7

Change Your Story

*"If you're searching for that one person who will
change your life... take a look in the mirror."*
- Unknown

You have everything you need within you to change your story. You are in control of your life. You have more power than you could ever know. We have talked about everything you need to make today the first day of the rest of your life. The key is accepting the simplicity in which you can change your story. It is simply daily actions that get you where you want to go. The key there is action, not words.

You can talk about where you are going to go. You can talk about what you are going to do. You can talk about why, who or what is keeping you from your hopes and dreams. The truth is: all of that is bullshit. The significant changes in life come from action. It is making the decision to accept your story and the decision to change your story that gives you the permission to take action. After you have made those decisions you take daily action towards your goals. You take daily actions to make your story the way you want it to be.

The biggest shift in my life occurred when I made the decision to change my story with my mental health. I blamed everything and everyone else. I felt hopeless. I felt ashamed. Anxiety and panic attacks were defining me in a negative way. The moment I decided to change that is the moment my life started to shift positively. Was the shift instant? Not even close. There was one instant change and that was the way I felt instantly after making the decision to take control and to take action.

There is something so invigorating when you decide to put everything on you. To take responsibility for everything that happens to you and how you react to it. We have been trained by ourselves and others our entire lives how to point the finger and focus on external factors. The beauty is we can change that with a flip of a switch because it is on us to make it on us. No one can make us not take responsibility. That is under our control. Taking responsibility for everything will take a hell of a lot of practice and a hell of a lot of discipline, but you can do it, I know you can.

One of the biggest factors in whether or not you will succeed in this is constant reminders to yourself of what you are trying to do. One great action step is to put items or post-its that remind you certain things that you are trying to change. For example, you can put a post-it on your bathroom mirror that says "Tell Your True Story." You would see it everyday and it would a constant reminder to analyze if you are living your genuine true story. It can also be an item you put on your desk at work and every time you see it you repeat a phrase to yourself such as, "I am enough" or "Be the change. Take action!".

I know these sound incredibly simple but we have already covered that change is simple, implementation is not. Imagine how your life would be if you had constant reminders of what you were trying to accomplish, how amazing you were, how you are in control and you are a badass mother fucker. Constant reminders on a daily basis to tell your true story, help others and take action towards things and humans that bring value to your life. These are all things that you have control over. You can put these reminders everywhere in your life and pretty soon that is what you start to become.

The universe brings back to you what you put out into it. If you are focusing on being you, knowing that you are enough, helping others, peace, love and positivity, that is what you will get in return. You can manifest who you want to become with your direction and action. I promise you that. The key again is taking responsibility and being consistent with the action necessary to get you to where you want to go and change your story.

Your story is yours. You are in control. You are beautiful. You are fucking unstoppable. Tell your story the way you want it to be. Change your story to what you want it to be. If you start telling yourself your story the way you want it to be over and over and over, your story will start to change and you will be more happy and more fulfilled. That is a promise. Make the commitment for yourself and everyone around you that today is the day. You will begin to change your story with your simple actions starting right now. You will take ownership of your story and decide what attributes you want it to have. You will love everything about yourself and fight like hell to improve not only yourself but to help others improve themselves as well. You will BE THE CHANGE!

China McCarney

CHAPTER 8
One Final Story

"Your life is your story. Write well. Edit often."
- Susan Statham

As this journey of this book comes to a close I want to thank you for reading my perspective on my story and the importance of telling your story. The key words there are "my perspective". This book is not based on clinical research or data. It is based on my life experience and what I have seen that has lead to people being successful. In reality, that may be those important data of all: life experience. Our stories are constantly evolving and changing and we have to be ok with making changes for improvement.

Think back to ten years ago or even five years ago and analyze how much you have changed and evolved. It is incredible right? Now analyze what has lead to the most impactful changes or most successful changes. My guess is the changes you cherish the most are the ones you had to work towards with action, the ones you had to challenge yourself to get out of your comfort zone, or the ones you did for yourself even when people did not agree with the changes you were going to make. The changes we cherish the most are the ones we have ownership over. The ones that move us closer to being our genuine selves.

A final story I want to share regarding my mental health journey with anxiety and panic attacks is a little more in-depth look at the last three year window. Going from sitting in a car after a panic attack feeling hopeless and at rock bottom, to sitting here today in my apartment in Manhattan Beach, CA owning a house in Arizona and getting close to completing my second book in 2 years. In the last three years I have published two books, started a podcast, founded the Athletes Against Anxiety and Depression foundation, bought a house, earned three raises and have helped the company I work for quintuple in size. That in no way is boasting or bragging and I can hear some of you as you read that say "this fucking guy". This is to prove the point of the theme of this book.

You see, the physical symptoms or mental health has not improved dramatically in the last three years. In fact, there are times when I feel like my panic attacks and anxiety are worse now than before. There are times I can't go into a grocery store. There are times that I am at an awesome event and feel like I need to run for the door or I am going to pass out. I am the same guy physically today that I was three years ago. What has changed? The mentality that I will go through a fucking wall with action before I let anxiety and panic attacks keep me from living a great life and keep me from helping others.

That is all that changed. I decided I was going to BE THE CHANGE instead of letting anxiety change my story in a negative way. I decided that I was going to take 100% responsibility for what occurred in my life and 100% responsibility for any of the changes I wanted to see. I wanted to write a book so I wrote a book. I wanted to start a podcast so I started a podcast. On and on and on.

The part that was the most eye-opening when I first started

to take the action was that nothing was impossible. Simple sentence but what do I mean? I, like most of us, looked at certain things with hopeless eyes and didn't know where to start. I didn't know the first thing about podcasting, I didn't have a microphone and there is no way I could edit and produce it. I thought of all the reasons why the task was hopeless and why I wasn't qualified. And then, action. I took the first small action of Googling how to podcast. Talked to people I know in my network that had done something similar. Found someone that would edit and produce the shows and put them on iTunes. Small action after small action and the Pursuit of Perfection Podcast was launched.

The final result (the podcast being launched) came because of small action after small action. The final result came because I was not afraid to ask for help and to seek others that were smarter than me that could point me in the right direction. Was it easy? Hell no. But it was exhilarating to see what my mindset was at square one compared to where it was upon completion.

Another misconception that I had, and I think a lot of people have, is that successful people aren't terrified when they first start out or even when they are established. "They just have a gift" or "They're just lucky they don't get nervous". False. If you do the research, and find interviews and conversations with most highly successful people, almost all of them mention either being terrified at the beginning or still getting nervous during performances. They are after all, humans. The difference between them and most average people is they make the decision to take action, tell their own story, and pursue what they really want and who they want to be.

Make that decision. Define what you want. Define who you

want to be. Manifest that person and tell your story the way you want it to be told. You have all the ingredients for your best recipe inside of yourself. The beautiful thing is you will gain new ingredients your entire life as well. The cycle never stops. You will constantly grow, constantly learn and constantly improve if you live openly and are willing to fight and take action. You are capable of anything that you want in this life. Be you, ALL of YOU!

Tell Your Story. Accept Your Story. Your Story Matters. Accept Other's Stories. Be The Change.

Tell Your Story

China McCarney

Acknowledging Those In My Story

"Don't worry about being acknowledged by others; worry about failing to acknowledge them."
- Confucius

My story is only my story because of the contributions of so many in my life. We can get so caught up in the craziness of day to day life that we fail to acknowledge the ones we love as much as we should. Make that an action that is a priority to you in your life as well. Acknowledge those that add value to your life and add value to theirs as well.

First and foremost my pops John. You have always been my rock and the man I look up to more than any other. You have laid the foundation of my story with your story and I appreciate the hell out of the fact that I am blessed to be your son. His wife, and my step-mother Barbara. Without your influence I would be nowhere near the man I am today. You came into our lives at just the right time and without you I would be a terrible negotiator and dress like your husband dressed himself before you came along. You two have provided such incredible guidance and continue to do so. Thank you.

To my mom Loretta, my sister Jennifer and my grandma Marie. You three generations of women in our family have always been an important part of my life and my story. We have shared incredible memories and have learned incredible lessons based on all of our journeys. I hope this book makes you proud.

To Jerry McCarney and Jason Burton. You guys have continued to pursue your passion and tell your story your way. Thank you for being more than family and inspiring me to continue to push boundaries.

To some of my first mentors: Jim and Bob Harmon, Joey Scarbury, Sheila Cook, Steve Pinkston, Joe Perez, Jon Sisco, Bob James, Jerry Koopman, Tim Jorgenson, Ken Brown, Chris Cota, Billy Picketts, Coach Smitty and Mark "Frank" Kertenian. All of you impacted my story and taught me something that has stuck with me to this day.

To the two men that gave me the beginning of my professional career; Alan Jaeger and Jim Vatcher. Alan, I will be forever grateful for your mentoring and guidance. Jim, the day-to-day life would be nowhere near the same without you and I am so glad we have evolved over the years battling in the trenches together.

To the amazing humans that I am lucky enough to have on my team:

Aubrey Mable, your soul is unmatched on this earth and I am the luckiest human to have you in my life. Your effect on me in such a short time is incredible and I can't wait to see what the future holds.

Tim Dixon, you made an instant impact on my life the first day I saw you give a speech. I still live many of those principles on a daily basis and I am so thankful we are on a podcast journey and just starting our professional story together.

Scott Morris, your passion for leaving an impact on this earth and helping others is absolutely incredible. As you say, "Your Team Matters" and I am lucky to be on your team.

Zach Cole, the man that makes dreams come true. No book, no podcast, no foundation comes to life without your visions, your talents and your creativity.

Jon Spendlove, one conversation kept me going on a path to changing my story with my mental health. I will be forever grateful for your encouragement. You've helped me continue on a path to help others and there is no greater gift.

There is no way I have named everyone that has impacted my story. It would be impossible to list everyone by name. If you have been a part of my story you can smile knowing I appreciate you and you helped my story get to where it is today. I acknowledge you and I encourage everyone to acknowledge those in your story as often as possible.

To the next chapter of this story and this life, I will never stop trying to be the change for myself and for everyone in my story. No let's take action and get to work....

China McCarney

Made in the USA
Middletown, DE
24 February 2018